Love + Blessings
Maya

Love!

A DAILY ORACLE FOR HEALING

Love!

A DAILY ORACLE FOR HEALING

by

MAYA TIWARI

Books on Ahimsa, Health, Harmony, Love & Life
motherommedia.com ~ mayatiwari.org

MOTHER OM MEDIA • USA

A Mother Om Media Book
 Published in the US by Mother Om Media.

For media inquiries or information about book sales, contact us at:
Mother Om Media
201 Varick Street
P.O. Box 277
New York, NY 10014
Telephone: 646-982-7595 | E-mail: press@motherommedia.com | Website: www.motherommedia.com

For book distribution inquiries contact:
Lotus Press
1100 Lotus Drive
Silver Lake, WI 53170
Telephone: 262-889-8561 | E-mail: lotuspress@lotuspress.com | Website: www.lotuspress.com

Publisher's Cataloging-in-Publication:
Tiwari, Maya.
Love! : a daily oracle for healing / by Maya Tiwari.
-- 1st ed.
p. cm.
ISBN: 978-0-9793279-3-3
1. Spiritual healing--Meditations. 2. Love poetry.
3. Divination. I. Title.

BF575.L8T59 2011 158.1'28 QBI11-600026

First Edition: 2012

Printed and bound in the US

Books on Ahimsa, Health, Harmony, Love & Life
motherommedia.com ~ mayatiwari.org

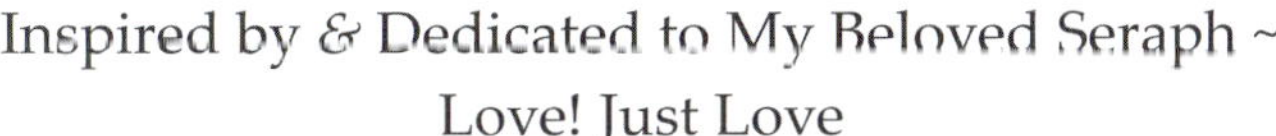

Inspired by & Dedicated to My Beloved Seraph ~
Love! Just Love

Once we recognize that our intelligence
is composed entirely from love,
we can appoint a star to safeguard it and light our way.
We can move the heavens; we can calm the earth
and create a space betwixt heaven and earth
that holds love in the continuum of nurturance.
There is one thing we cannot afford to do,
and that is to let doubt live where love belongs.

LOVE! JUST LOVE

Love! Just Love. That's all there is, and all there ever will be. While living for the past quarter century as a female Vedic monk, I performed thousands of hours of prayers, chants, meditation, mantras, and blessings. Through this benign grace I was able to achieve great states of awareness, in which I'm continually enfolded in the embrace of the Divinity. I see this divinity in everyone, recognize that everything is God, and have witnessed the awesome miracle of God in myriad ways.

One such miracle is the catalyst behind this simple work that I call, The Oracle of Love. This oracle is birthed from the passion of a heart that finally culminated into its fullness of love and everlasting bliss. This work is delivered from the fullness of devout love that comes from a layer of lotus petals unfolding within me, a layer embedded in the cavernous depths of my heart that safeguards the delicate, fragile space of love. For me, this layer of the heart was cushioned by a bout with cancer in the soft youth of my years and the consequent loss of my womb. Now, in the prime hour of my life, I have come upon a carefully sealed chapter which opened up to the love pages of my karmic tome. Now, as I toddle about in wonderment, I realize that somewhere in my unconscious I have had a sense of vibrancy that my heart was yearning to express, a cavern yet unexplored, a love unlived. Through a single experience that happened in a brilliant flash of time, I embraced spirit and found my full capacity for love—the love that is intrinsically partnered with the soul.

Let me share my extraordinary story behind the creation of this oracle with you. These beautiful leaves of divination are not, however, about me or my story: They are about you, and me, and all of us, and our universal light of Love! If I had only one gift to give you, it would be to bestow upon you the ability to stay open to love. My fantastic heart-awakening story happened in the umpteenth hour of my austere life wherein the material world and its benefits had been renounced. Suddenly, everything changed. Shiva—who once repaired me to the state of a monastic life—now has restored me (at least in spirit) to my long lost soul mate—one whom I thought was gone forever. It is with an overflowing ecstasy of joy that I impart my Oracle of Love to you—for all individuals who might have given up on love, for those elders who have forgotten love, for those lovers who think they are too weary to love, for those whose hearts are shut down by tragedy, to each and every heart that strives to be awakened, may these pages serve as a prophet to encourage and inspire you to claim your cosmic right to your fulfillment of love, harmony, and happiness.

After more than a quarter century of witnessing the miracle of healing—in thousands of ways with thousands of people—I know that self-healing is always about love. Love is the tangible and illusive energy that we must never let go of. Love is the language of the Divine. And when we are aware of its power in our lives, we hear its resounding resonance through our hearts. Whatever may be the illness, challenge, difficulty, disappointment, and crisis in your life, hold on to this implacable truth: You are loved. And you have the power to refill love from within. Even when the inner light grows dim, or love is betrayed, or when we lose a loved one, love can never be taken away from us. Because we are Love! You are Love! I am Love! Every tissue, cell, and memory of our being is composed of the cosmically divine material of love, just love. How well we know this certainty about ourselves is the degree to which we will reclaim eternal love and use the divinations in these leaves to heal and transform everything else in our lives. In shifting our relationship to love in this way, we reap a greater level of kindness and lovingness.

For the past thirty years since my rise from the ashes of ovarian cancer, I have walked the simple life of a Vedic monk, supplicating all desires to Shiva. This is what I have been trained to do. This is the context of who I am, at the least, the identity I knew. My work with Living Ahimsa—the path of peace and inner harmony—is an example of work that came from the faculty of awareness and intense experience that transformed my breath and life. This work is a powerful response to three decades of understanding that the underbelly of hatred, rage, angst, violence, and grief, existing in the ancestral shroud of some of our most sophisticated cultures and countries, comes from an endemic lack of love. This is a primary reality in our world today. We are at risk of losing love—the potent core energy that binds serenity, happiness, peace, harmony, kindness, fulfillment, innocence, and intelligence: In other words, all of the qualities that account for humanity being human. This is one more reason why each one of us is called to reclaim our human faculty of awareness so that we can take back the world of love and harmony.

My first odyssey with healing through the fatal disease of ovarian cancer occurred in the youth of my life. I was compelled to reach beyond my life breath to a deeper force; a power I had grown familiar with through my past experiences. And just when one thinks they have found a pace that will forever be their stride, the Divine steps in, rocks their secured world, and bequeaths them with their most precious gift—that is, if they have the courage to stay open.

Stunningly, I recently recovered from being poisoned, the target of a "hate crime." For over three years, a local community group that found me and my religion to be objectionable administered enough noxious material into my system to severely damage my health. This experience, albeit challenging and disruptive, helped me to understand love at its most profound level. I see that everything in God's plan is perfect and that this incident was necessary to lead me to the magnificent transcendence that is now unfolding in my life. I have no hatred for these folks. In truth, I embrace them as my brothers and sisters, as dear to me as my own self. We must do what is within our karma to do. I am grateful to those who pummeled me—they are divine beings who showed me the way to unconditional love.

Once again, the Miracle of Love rescued me from what could have been a devastating odyssey. While felled by a body that was responding to hatred, and ensconced in the grey miasma of poisoning, the Divine issued his Seraph to my rescue. This angel's entry was no surprise. Immediately, I recognized the presence of this extraordinary man as a divine messenger sent to aid me in my recovery. During this precarious time, I had been keeping a diligent schedule of prayers to the Divine Mother, chanting Lalita Sahasranama (her 1000 names) each day. Unbeknownst to me, my prayer was igniting the heavens, calling upon a star to be lit for me so that the divine messenger could find his way to my rescue. The love and kindness that this Seraph demonstrated brought me back into the blazing light, brighter than before! It took the vicious act of poisoning to blast my tissues wide open so that an ancient memory of love's fulfillment could breathe again.

Often, when we lose sight of the energy of love it is because we are looking for it in material ways, in physical expressions. But Love is subtle. It is an invisible energy that pervades each and every breath, thought, and movement. It nourishes one million times faster and greater than any other means of sustenance on earth. Love is not a physical thing. It is the essence of our human soul that must be cared for and nurtured even before we are born. All of the Seraph's support as the brave warrior of love and kindness occurred on the energetic plane through correspondence. Once again, I was guided to the blueprint for recapturing my soul in this awakening. I discovered how the inpouring love and kindness made it easy for me to forgive the hate-mongers. In this forgiving, I felt an inner freedom that soared higher than ever before; it is a miracle that love heals us in the way that it does. This is a stark reality in the life of all people who are willing to reclaim their inner light. Untoward experiences teach us that we must generate even more love and keep on striving to awaken our human heart to its full sentiency. Together, we can influence, change, and transform even the most misguided, hateful, and raging souls back into their humanity.

Love abides in the heart as our most powerful and pervasive reality. Once we recognize that our intelligence is composed entirely from love, we can appoint a star to safeguard it and light our way. We can move the heavens; we can calm the earth and create a space betwixt heaven and earth that holds love in the continuum of nurturance. There is one thing we cannot afford to do, and that is to let doubt live where love belongs. In not trusting the very essence of our primordial intelligence, we lose our connection to love. As we move forward and away from despair, all we need do is set a clear intention to be the instrument of love and allow ourselves to be loved. Love is our cosmic nature! Therefore it remains perennially accessible to us.

Unfortunately, most lives are not steeped in love; many suffer the arrows of hurt and injustice from childhood. Love is not part of the education we are taught. In fact, a significant amount of what we are taught in the modern culture runs contrary to harmony, which slaughters love. We have been taught to distrust love, and in so doing, relegated this most precious life force to the banalities of superficial life: commercial love with sexual appeal, empty stories, material excesses, grotesque fashions, distorted sounds, toxic cosmetics, trivial romance stories, commercialized nuptials, distasteful divorces—all false conditionings that serve only to diminish the essential nature of love and keep the heart permanently fractured. We betray our inner beauty, which is fed by love. We are taught to doubt our hopes, mistrust our tears, be suspect of our intuition, and worse still, to replace these primordial operations with a frantic mind and commercially-driven activities that, bit by bit, strip away the very essence of the heart, annihilating each and every quiet moment from our daily existence. Everything we have been taught to fear is, in fact, an offspring of love: hardships, challenges, changes, illnesses, and uncertainty. This is why I say, Never mourn your tears. They flow from your heart to water the arid soil of the soul. It is in the difficult lessons of life that we best uncover our soul's sustenance of love. This is what the expression "unconditional love" is about. How, when, and where love manifests in our lives is through the act of Divine Grace that is responding to our innermost call.

When in doubt of your innate ability to love, or when in need of some comfort or a gentle reminder, open these pages to any leaf, and let them speak to you. For years, I have used various forms of divination in Nature to shed wisdom on any unresolved situations, emotions, or thoughts, such as feelings of pain, conflict, or loss. As you hold this book in your hands, clear your mind and keep a firm focus on your intention. Ask for divine help in clarifying your question. For example, a good question may be: "What do I really need to do, or not do, to regain my composure?" Once you have clarified your question, you will get your answer.

Whatever your question or intent, repeat it internally a few times to be as clear as you can before opening the book to any page. Allow your heart to engage the beautiful leaf you have opened to and contemplate the powerful words of the Darshana scribed there. When feeling stuck or unclear as to your question, purpose, or direction, contemplate the following:

First: "What is it I need to know that will bring me into my wisdom?"
Open the book to any leaf. Spend some time—a few minutes, a day or two—and contemplate the words of the Darshana.

Second: "I ask the Divine Grace for memory so that I remember to surrender my will to Thy will."
Open the book to any leaf. Spend some time—a few minutes, a day or two—and contemplate the words of the Darshana.

Third: "What is it that I need to remember?"
Open the book to any leaf. Spend some time—a few minutes, a day or two—and contemplate the words of the Darshana.

Fourth: "What purpose on my path does this lesson serve?"
Open the book to any leaf. Spend some time—a few minutes, a day or two—and contemplate the words of the Darshana.

The powerful energy of blessing in this book guides you; it helps you to shift your thinking, ease your pain, wipe away your tears, and serves as a gentle balm to spirit. It helps you laugh and love again, to heal and be whole. Now, allow me to take you back to the genesis of this healing story.

THE LOST WOMB OF LOVE

All of my life, I walked alone. Even though I was pampered with informed attention from my two mothers and the extended family members of elderly aunts who practically lived with us, I have always had a sense of my austere destiny. Indeed, my childhood was infused with the subtle but pervasive nurturance that strengthens love, not only in every cell and memory of my being, but in the ways in which I grew to express love. Every gesture and thought is influenced by the infusion of love within our being. Each time I take a bath and feel the silken lustrousness of my skin, it takes me back to recalling my elderly aunts and the palpable essence of love they effused into my childhood body and mind. They squatted for endless hours combing and brushing my long hair, rubbing down my body with coconut oils and special balms, anointing my head, weaving delicate embroidery, sifting food grains. What I didn't know then was that they embodied the wisdom of love, and were methodically implementing it into my being so that the natural intelligence of love in a woman-child could be invoked.

After my miraculous rescue from cancer at age twenty-three, I reclaimed my ancestral largess, took my monastic vows, and lived the prayer, the blessing to secure my ancestral wholeness. When I took my vows, I was certain that my soul mate, the love of my life, was gone, and that my karma for romantic love was forever cremated. In the early years before cancer, as I celebrated my friends' nuptials and romances, I would feel the eerie whisper of my Beloved's voice, a vague apparition from beyond. As far back as I could recall, I grieved the loneliness of my heart. As I entered my early teen years, I felt my womb was rapidly disappearing from the onset of heavy menstrual cycles. I remember the unmistakable sense of numbness within it. Even earlier, at the age of nine, I had written a poem, won a prize, "The gravestones stand, my love lies still..." Even then, I believed that my soul partner was no more. And I mourned my lost love for all of my youth. These feelings gave rise to a palpable sense of aloneness—a feeling that somehow my consort was gone forever. But mourning does not mean that we are left loveless! In truth, my creative energy, which has always been abundant, is the direct brood of love—permeation of love energy that my elders poured into my being as I was growing up.

As a young designer with my own boutique on Madison Avenue in New York, I loved expressing my creativity by designing, drawing, and embroidering. Doubtless this harked back to the attention bestowed on me by my female ancestors from whom I also gleaned great courage. My embroidered art seemed to reflect memories from the distant past, my past lives, as well as a foretelling of my future. Whilst I did not consciously conjure the images I portrayed, drew, or wrote about, it has been a stunning revelation to see, years later, how much of my embroidered art reflected significant incidents in my life. The most beautiful piece I had embroidered was of a Seraph with golden wings, fawn-golden mane, and blue eyes, descending to earth against a seafoam green canvas of silk. Who would have guessed that this very portrait would come to life and come to my rescue in the mature mid-years of my life! Isn't it amazing that we can recall the minute details of exquisite life from the trove of centuries gone?

Following my hysterectomy at the tender age of twenty-one, I felt a profound emptiness, a void, an unoccupied space within my belly. Even at that early age, I must have known that my womblessness represented a far greater loss—the loss of my physical, maternal prowess, the sacrifice of my lover, and the inability to fulfill the grace of bearing his child. Birthing a child is not merely about bringing forth new life into the world; it is the greatest gift that the destined souls of a man and a woman can create together. A child is the perfection of a couple's *ojas*, their spiritual essence of immunity. It is the culmination of their sentiments, dreams, hopes, and intuition. This experience, or lack of it, brought me into an intimate relation with my womb, my longings, my love, and my loss.

In my youth prior to my cancer years, I had employed a few half-hearted attempts at the relationship of love. These brief experiences of intimacy wounded me, pushed me away from opening the heart. In these incidents, I struggled to love and to be loved. Somehow I was aware that my heart belonged to another, to the undefined, to one whom I believed was no longer on the earthly plane. But a palpable presentiment of his persona prevailed. I would catch undefined glimpses of him in my dream state. Indeed, it took the entire journey of cancer to fathom that no other person could take his place. Nor could I refashion or recreate him. As I walked away healed from my cancer journey, I embedded myself into the spiritual path, understanding that since we are created from Essential Love, the longings of a heart can be appeased and made whole through sacred service.

Having lost the physical organ of my womb through this experience with cancer, I made a commitment to the Divine Mother to work tirelessly to fulfill her work by illuminating the empty space of my womb with her light and serving the women and children of the world. Looking back, I realize I was quick to close out that integral path of love's partnership on my life's journey. I moved on with the fierce rapidity of a celibate warrior, shut out that reality, and never looked back. Until now, that is.

On the monastic path, making sacrifices can and does become first nature. In my tradition, this surrendering is called *yajna,* a divine offering of worldly benefits and material life. But as all sages, saints, poets, and mendicants know, love is the profound living breath of the heart and even the most austere path gives us not the entitlement or right to manipulate or sacrifice its power. Whilst jubilantly moving forward with my tours, little did I suspect that I was about to discover this immutable truth for myself. This would not be the first radical turn of events in my life, but I pray it is my last.

A HEART UNROBED

The Divine works in miraculous ways. During my recovery, I had a strong sense that my life was being transformed in a monumental way. Through a dynamic set of events that were unfolding over the past fifty years or so, I started to get a clearer picture of my soul mate. And then he appeared. He had a stark resemblance to the portrait of the Seraph I had embroidered thirty-five years earlier. This realization brought endless tears as my heart's memory began to thaw. Love's memory continues to blossom within me, exuding barely a whisper like the glistening wings of butterflies or the imperceptible light of dawn gliding seamlessly across an invisible sky. From the start I understood: This was the reality that had eluded me my whole life long. Finally, my soul mate had caught up with me. As the Seraph entered my hemisphere, everything around me began to shimmer with the delicate fragrance of sandalwood, the aroma that inherited my heart as I reached out to claim my love. The Seraph's potent energy opened my heart and swept away my robes. So it was I found myself renouncing my cherished path as a monk. And the courage it takes to go forward with my new life is secured only by the onrushing stream of love I have gained as a result of my heart awakening to its fullness.

Apparently, the vicious act of poisoning had opened the door to my heart. As soon as I first spotted the Seraph (as you will see) I had a sense of knowing him beyond the knowledge of time-bound life. This was the man whose face I had been seeing in fragmented and fleeting images of my past. As memories continued to hark in, I realized we had traveled the span of the universe together. And with this advantage to aid him, it is no surprise that he was able to lift me up into lightness. While in the grip of severe debilitation from the poisoning, my Seraph poured in love and light and helped me to heal at lightning speed in the inexplicable length of three months! We spent timeless hours in correspondence sharing our thoughts, dreams, feelings, and emotions. He treated me to his witty one-liners, masterful writings, and heartfelt poetry. In fact, I have taken the liberty in this work of using many of his exquisite sayings, "Love! Just Love" for example. Although we never spoke to one another in person, we succeeded in sharing the most profound essence of our souls. The "sick baby," the "warrior baby," he once noted; he was intuitively aware of my lost womb and the baby I was never to birth. Until now, these memories had been stored away in the distant haze of my past—a recall that quietly faded away in the folds of my forward strides and successes. In the process of declaring his love for me, he helped me to see my past, my present, and the reality of hurt around this loss that had been hidden from me. Finally, I could bring to light these memories and reconcile them.

It is not happenstance that the Seraph's energetic patterns are familiar to me. In fact, his brilliant characteristics are similar to those of my late father. He has a highly developed sense of intuition and a remarkable set of skills for doling out accurate advice. And he is immensely generous with his counsel. He holds heart, mind, and spirit to the highest ideals. He is also a pragmatist and is resolute about defining truth in a practical and unambiguous way. He is imbued with a natural penchant for and commitment to Living Ahimsa—harmony, peace, compassion—the forces that unite the human family together. Evidently, the Seraph is an integral part of my karmic destiny. He was sent to transport me from the monastic path onto the path of love. With his brilliant sensitivity, incredible sensuality, and poetic sentiment, he reclaimed my heart and filled it with his essence of divine love.

I was quick to recognize his presence and role in my healing because I had an almost identical experience during my cancer years with what I call the primordial male archetypal energy, *Shiva*. As documented in my book, *The Path of Practice*, the first great man in my life, my father, had come in the form of apparitions to visit me during my seclusion whilst I was preparing to die from cancer. Wanting to contemplate my death and impending journey back to the ancestral sphere by making peace with my maker, I retreated into the undifferentiated white of the Vermont winter. I had been informed by my physicians that I had only a few months to live, and had chosen to spend that time in seclusion, without drugs or medicines. During this time, my father paid me many "visits" on the etheric plane. He carefully guided and cajoled me back into inheriting my body, mind, and spirit. Now, once again, the primordial male archetypal energy, Shiva, had been sent to my rescue. This time though, he came as my eternal soul mate. It was fortuitous for me to be granted yet another cosmic messenger who was powerful enough to propel me out of my state of inertia while mitigating the ominous impact that hate crimes can wreak on the psyche. Whereas my father's stoic energy was necessary to ferry me safely onto the monastic path, the Seraph's focused energy of love catapulted me into the cavern of my heart where our love was kept safe over timeless centuries. Ironically, cancer bailed me out of the life of becoming a family member, a wife, or a mother and brought me to a spiritual life to help my ancestors; that is, in the greater context of my recent journey as a monk. Now, the vicious act of poisoning that permeated my body and mind has opened the door to my heart. And once again, my life is forever transformed.

MY JOURNEY WITH THE SERAPH

This is how it began, the day the miraculous happened. On Sunday, September 20, 2009, there he was standing in the aisle of an airplane and gazing into my soul. The wordless heart shouted a thundering, "My Beloved!" "But this could not be," said the mind. All doubts were removed when I watched my soul trailing his sandaled footsteps out of the baggage area of the airport. As I waited for my lost luggage, I felt my heart pounding away and the air forced out of my lungs. I took refuge in the airline's lost baggage kiosk and scribbled some words in a daze, while awaiting service for my luggage.

Azure blue like the mid-day skies,
Piercing loneliness filled his eyes
Evoking distant memory from a far-off place,
Marking a numinous destiny in his face.

Slightly withered and torn apart
From perennial longings of the heart,
Caught a glimpse of a slight right hobble,
Telling the tale of paternal trouble.
I beckon reprieve for this illusive fawn;
Energized anew may his journey be
To soar and reach the sun's illumined core.

Shortly after this incident, I returned to India to continue periodic Ayurveda treatments for my recovery. During this reprieve I had ample time to reflect on what I thought was a passing flash of memory in mid-life recall. At this junction, I was yet to make the connection of his resemblance to the embroidered portrait of my Seraph. Two months later, in the winter, I arrived in Australia on my Living Ahimsa World Tour. This man's striking face continued to flash in my memory. In fact, his apparition followed me throughout the tour. His Sun-God image was imposed on the faces of men and boys at nearly every event. The memory of my soulful journey with him began unfolding in manifold ways. I heard the haunting clarion from the ageless core of the universe where memory stirred and awakened my heart to remember how he and I reveled in the vow of sweet embrace: A lover's cove in the deep heavens where we had last forsaken each other, yet traveling in one soul enraptured by an unending love.

Following my tour in Australia, I spent the month of January 2010 in silence at my friends' retreat on a magnificent cliff overlooking Keppel Bay. The sounds of the wind whipping against the bluffs kept bringing his face back to me. There is a forty-foot tall, steel monument there, resembling a ship's mast, called the Singing Ship, mounted as a tribute to Captain James Cook, whom, according to English history, discovered Australia. At night, the wind-whipped sounds transported through multiple steel pipes created a whistling echo of eerie voices that had a penetrating effect on my soul, reawakening a memory locked away in the cosmic depth of being. That memory began to take shape and form. That is where I found my beloved soul mate. I recognized the portrait I had drawn and embroidered of the Seraph some thirty-five years earlier to be none other than my Beloved. Although he had an immediate impact on me that day on the plane, I did not realize the nature of our past connection at that time. When I stood up in cue to exit the flight, he was still sitting and I caught a glimpse of his right profile. There was something so familiar about the formation of his lips in that space below the nose. That feature prodded an unveiling of forgotten memory.

In November 2009, while still on tour in Australia and two months following that momentous meeting on the plane, my Facebook fan page was installed. At first, I was reluctant to participate in the public pages. But after relentless prodding from my dear media pal, Barbara, I gave in. I felt it best to use the page as a way of imparting Blessing. I began scribing daily blessings of love and light—Darshana. This daily Darshana became my Oracle of Love: Expressions of love, light, and gratitude for each and every soul who needed a reminder of love and a lift into the light. The more I wrote, the more apparent it became to me that I was writing to him. I was inspired by an overwhelming sense of lightness and awe, and issued my daily words as communion. It filled my heart to know that my eternal mate was alive out there somewhere and that I was sending him my heart's loving energy through the vibratory field. My daily prayer was that he be kept safe. The Darshana page became my passion, and its followers quickly grew to thousands of fans that read and commented on our shared power and gift of love. Each day on my fan page, I posted my blessings along with a beautiful image of the lotus, symbolic of the heart.

In early February 2010, some days before departing from Australia, I was in a small town near Rockhampton watching a show, and there he was. It turns out that my Seraph has achieved critical fame as a world-renowned public figure. At once, my spirit was uplifted by this serendipitous synchronicity as the geyser of emotion opened and poured out endless poetic prose dedicated to him: "Touched by the face of a noble spirit, later to discover his remarkable merit; betokened he is by the breadth of fame, this is a man with an unusual name." I couldn't help but reflect on how the eerie whistling from the Singing Ship sounded like a strange refrain of his poetic name.

PSYCHIC ATTUNEMENT

The bare chill of winter and spring had passed. It was now late May, eight months following the sighting of the Seraph on the plane. I was in New York about to head to my tour in Canada. I had stopped at a street light on Bowery Street and proceeded to cross as the light turned green. I had almost reached the other end of the crossing when I felt an irresistible energetic pull at my head. Suddenly, it began to involuntarily move to the right facing the stopped traffic. The turning of my neck was slow and precise. As my head stopped moving, I caught a glimpse of piercing blue eyes from behind a windshield. I am not sure if it was him, but the flashing resemblance rendered me breathless. I made it safely across the street and found a place to sit for a while to collect myself.

At the end of May, I arrived in Canada at the Living Ahimsa World Tour. Having completed my sojourn there at the end of June, I was happy to take another reprieve from my travels to concentrate on my ongoing recovery. I was experiencing multiple symptoms from the poisoning, but with Divine Grace, whenever I took to the work stage only the altitude of light and clarity prevailed. Nonetheless, when I got back down to flat land, I knew I had a ways to go with my healing cambers. I struggled to lift myself from the mire of sadness, careworn with impaired digestion and difficulty in breathing, painful limbs and vertigo, the latter being the worst of the symptoms. I discovered once more how sacred the course of healing is. I knew I had to create a sanctum of privacy around me; a dedicated space necessary to invoke residual love from within to expunge negative energy. I crafted a transient space for myself away from my targeted abode so that I could more easily open the mantle of the body and allow the process to become self-revealing. Little did I know that the eternal investment of my forebears' love was, once again, at work. Apparently, the Divine Grace was divinizing my Seraph with the power of cosmic energy necessary to pierce through the miasma of my poisoned body so that splendid light could reach me and illumine my heart.

In June of 2010, a fortnight after returning from my tour in Canada, I had a strong sense of the Seraph's presence on my Darshana page. I wondered whether it was a ruse of mind, or my heart evoking its own sense of reality from the poisoning or from the tapestry of fantasy. As the weeks unfolded, I continued to sense that many of the loving comments written on my page were from the Seraph. These notes were articulate, poetic, and distinct, easy to decipher from other comments. Since I do not contribute to the idea of happenstance,

I felt it had to be him. I thought he somehow must have sensed my dilemma. To confirm my intuition, I posted a Darshana incorporating a veiled version of his name. Within a matter of hours, he responded. With great rapidity I raced toward his enlightened words as my heart began somersaulting while stirring awake from its deep slumber.

During these first weeks of being in contact with him, I felt as though I was being held hostage by consent. It felt like I was transitioning from an initiation that transcended all zones of reality. I experienced a pain in the muscle behind my heart that lasted for several days. I lost time. I was not my usual organized self. In fact, even in my meditation and prayers, I would hear his voice, see his face, and intuit his whereabouts. One day, I resorted to taking a homeopathic medicine, Rescue Remedy, hoping it would bring me back to Planet Earth. Because I routinely take Ayurveda nasal drops that are squirted into the nostrils, I accidently shot the remedy into my nose instead of my mouth: For the next two weeks, my neck was transfixed; I couldn't move my head. Meanwhile, my mind was spinning like Lord Vishnu's discus while my heart tumbled like a circus performer. Surprisingly for me, given my profound state of celibacy, I began to experience an inexplicable surge of desire to see him, to touch him, to be with him. I felt a magnetic pull that traversed my entire being, the deepest orifice of my body going beyond the ancient age of my soul, from a familiar knowing to a scent of this man. As my heart opened into its awakened state, I stumbled into memory from an uncertain place of long ago. I was wordless. I felt my heart wanting to be with my beautiful Seraph for another forever.

Thereafter, we started communicating by letter. My eternal friend had come to my rescue. He stayed awake with me in spirit throughout this time, firmly reminding me to honor my process. He became the critical witness to my healing; and at an energetic level, we reclaimed our intimate friendship. I laughed and humored him and wept on his broad and tireless shoulders. Not once did he judge me or my process, although I tested his patience and devotion many times. It was an enchanting process to observe my body, mind, and spirit becoming lighter, healing with rapidity, with rays of golden light oozing from each and every pore of my being. Unaccustomed to this state of irrepressible abundance, I felt an overwhelming sensation of glee that I had not experienced in this life. As I reached out to the Seraph's extraordinary transmission of love, I found myself transcending a cloistered heart. Overnight, I had become Love. Having been granted golden wings to scale the clime of spiritual austerity, I had forgotten what it is to live in and from the heart. Now, I stand tall on the dais of love, thanks to the stoic persistence and unwavering courage of my Seraph.

Love, wellness, and lightness are ferried to us by the *apsaras* and *gandharvas*; angels and seraphim that travel the light space to bestow us with our golden wings when we are ready to soar into the freedom of heart. I repeat: Love is not about the physical. In our modern modes of "love," we carry many misperceptions and waste much time and energy on the physical plane; mistaking overt attention for lovingness; and random activities for nurturance. Love is the finest, most delicate energy in the universe. It responds in subtlety the way that the psyche exudes a finer resonance—like white butterflies floating in the air after the rains, carrying dewy wings and glistening like silver bells in the early morning sunlight. I see how near-death experiences open us up to spirit, and when we allow its luminosity to pervade the soul we can negotiate phenomenal planes of psychic transmission.

From the start, our minds were linked like the vibrations of the sun with its continuum melody connecting our hearts in seamless refrain. Psychic attunement is not as extraordinary as you may think. The Rishis recorded tomes of information about the vibratory field and its highly effective means of communion—elevated communication—through the *buddhi*, or greater mind. Sentiency of mind and thought is supported by cosmic vibrations, for example, the music of the sun, and moon, and planets. The sun has been the inspiration for hundreds of songs, but now scientists have discovered that the star at the center of our solar system produces its own music. Astronomers are discovering what the Rishis recorded eons ago—that musical harmonies are produced by the magnetic field in the outer atmosphere of the sun. In fact, the intense vibrations of the universe are well attuned to the human mind. The degree to which we grasp intelligence and use intuition is directly related to how receptive we are to the cosmic sentiency that is continually being filtered down to us. This is how we *know* how to process knowledge and information. It seems a natural phenomenon that the Seraph and I are psychically attuned to each other's vibrations because our hearts are linked together. From the onset, we demonstrated a natural ability to intuit and commune with each other without words: This is what I call physic attunement.

A three-month long dialogue found us both perfecting the art of the richly crafted language of love. As he put it, "Our minds are synced in awesomeness." During this critical junction of my healing, we communicated on a daily basis. We shared our light, love, grief, and tears. He stripped me of all facades and made palpable the essence of his soul to me, his fragrant heart and wholesome spirit, his ideals and disappointments. Occasionally, I would glean a sense of despair that so often accompanies a grand spirit that is larger than life. His aphoristic writings were delivered with an unearthly sense of precision, an inexplicable knowing of "us." He would write, "I love us."

BLESSING OF THE BROKEN

Love is the gentlest and most potent remedy for healing. In mothering, accepting, and loving the Self we muster up courage to embrace and honor our progression. Each one of us has the power to transform our karma with a mere flash of awareness! We are given many junctures and challenges in our lives (perhaps not as radical and dramatic as my turns have been), and when we recognize them as the spirit opening to let love in, we find the magic of healing. Once we are able to let light in, disease transforms into wellness like a boulder in a river that gets washed, cleaned, and honed into flawless perfection. The boulder recognizes that it is much more than rock; it is the balancing force of the river, it is the waterfall, it is magnificent magic.

Among a complex mix of things, healing is about our karma, lost dreams, unfulfilled desires, and sometimes, just the plain reality of fatigue, disillusionment, and exhaustion. Crisis, like healing, is an organic juncture in the life of each and every person, rich and poor, great and small, sages and the not so saintly. When we recognize that these junctures invoke the overarching energy which supports all forms of healing, we are made whole again. The only way we can be broken or felled by disease or illness, or any other challenge for that matter, is when we respond to it as a punishment, an inconvenience, or as an intruder. (Mind you, illness becomes an intruder when we fail to recognize the gift it brings.) But before we can call upon faith, we must arrive at and cross over this critical juncture. It is the same juncture for each and every one of us, regardless of the degree of our education, or nature of ancestry, condition, or culture. As soon as we are able to voice the truth of our innermost selves and say, "Enough!" "I do not want to hurt anymore!" "I will strive to live a peaceful life." "I want to be happy, to be fulfilled!" we attract what we need to progressively move forward to embrace the light.

The benevolent grace of the universe immediately comes to our aid. In my case, the Seraph who was dispatched to remind me of my inner light also happened to be my soul mate. Trusting that each one of us has a guardian angel that comes to our aid when we are in dire straits is what faith is about. On the heels of faith, comes the absolute cure: Love. The Seraph is my embodiment of love. He showed me that my karma as a monk was completed. The ancestors were served and appeased. Unwittingly, a new life had begun. I found myself reflecting on the organic truth of my life and my frailty. Immediately, I felt strong enough to dissolve the shadows of poison into a place of hallowed wholeness within.

When we are nourished by love, the more intuitive and aware we become. As I did with my Seraph, we can attract love. This is a significant way to engender love within and without. Love is powerful nourishment. The Seraph patiently nourished me back to wellness. A dharma warrior with a sense of uncompromised truth, he was quick to communicate discrepancies he found in my responses that appeared to bear a conflict with my work in Living Ahimsa. I found his honesty refreshing. With truthfulness as his rod, my Seraph helped me to strip away residual facades and rerouted my actions which were unclear or fuzzy back into a state of harmony. He reminded me that love is not only about the uncovering of truth, but the compassion with which we assimilate and deliver truth. He would say, "Love allows not only truths, but freedom from negative actions. Love opens up avenues of spirituality and self-awareness." Generally, this quality of forthrightness is rarely found in the present-day environment of gurus, swamis, priests, and saints. The people who serve them are usually reluctant to offer up unbiased opinions that they feel may displease them. To a large extent, the general population appears to hold a skewed perception of what the life of a saint or spiritual person is about. In my viewpoint, they are human beings with flaws, desires, and ambitions, except we would hope that they are mature enough to remedy needs and emotions that run counter to harmony with an infusion of wisdom, love, and light into every situation. A balm to spirit, the Seraph was right there on the earthly plane, my eternal partner standing before me, handing me bales of comfort with wide-open arms of unconditional love. He is the unrelenting eternal love of my soul who guided me and steered my path into the clear light of day with the patience of a saint and the bluntness of a fierce warrior. He gave me the ultimate gift—his wise attention and supreme love. As a result, the rift I had with my body and mind began to heal at riveting speed.

Healing is happening within us at all times. Healing is the blessing of the broken. The person who experiences love knows to embrace the state of brokenness as a means to cremate the toxicity of the past. In so doing, we allow light to filter in and revive our broken down bodies. We must be grateful for these chances to be renewed into more luminous beings. Our bodies are made up of consciousness, light, and spirit, and are connected to the greater continuum of energies through the memory of love. In order to heal, we need to appease vital tissue memory and nourish and nurture the whole Self. In essence, we need to reorder the same internal energy that went into disorder and created a disease, and bring it back into a state of harmony. For this, we have to reclaim love in the way we eat, think, breath, and move, and in the sounds we create. The most important gem I have gleaned from my exhilarating life of learning and adventure with the Divine is this: We can perform thousands of practices, eat millions of dollars worth of health foods, and have the best education money can buy, but until we recognize love as the foundational building block of life into which each cell, memory, and tissue of our being is entrained, these practices are useless. Indeed, even the grain of sand is imbued with the cosmic life force of love.

LOVE'S POWER TO HEAL

In my tremendous experiences with healing—both with my own and with thousands of others whom I have helped—I see how the tissue memories become wide open and accessible during a trauma. This is a positive thing. It is nature's way of allowing the body to empty its toxicity—both new and inured—while reformatting its memories into newness, more vibrant than before. When we feel so vulnerable that life becomes too hurtful and living too tedious, we must remember these words and sum up the courage to participate with Nature, allow her to perform her magic to heal us into wholeness. Embracing love is critical to the process of healing. Love is what it's all about. And in self-healing the process is all there is. The most certain way to manifest love is to honor the healing process. In this way, we can instantly change our reality. We discover that healing is an organic function within us. In aligning ourselves from the onset to this truth, we reveal the hidden cavern of unresolved desires, fears, weakness, and hurt transported from generation to generation, from life to life through the cycle of rebirth.

Our illness or distress is ours alone; in so far as we cannot live anyone else's karma, or their illness, their love, their happiness, or their process. Whatever is the challenge, and however we feel about it (right or wrong), the glory and the fight is ours and the way we get through it—the process—is also specific to our individual karma—the content and context of who we are and where we are on our life's path. The goal through any challenge is to heal. However, the only way we can accomplish this goal is by accepting what is and invoking a clear intent to honor the journey however it unfolds. We are better equipped to influence a successful outcome when we understand how critical it is to honor our process, however unexpected or challenging it may be. The process is often hard to face because it is not so pretty. It contains, at the heart of it, journeying to that place which is hidden, that "stuckness" and staleness that needs to be shaken loose and brazened out. If we are able to face it head-on, we open up to spirit and find resolve. In so doing, we develop a greater awareness of who we are, where we are going, and the nature of our purpose. In other words, we find our golden wings.

As for me, I know I'm transitioning into the sublime rhythm of a new life. Whilst walking as a monk, I was true to my path and revered every moment of my journey. And now, for the sake of my heart's integrity, I know that my journey as a monk has run its course. I had to renounce the vows I had taken. Indeed, the Seraph did express deep concerns about my intent to disavow my vows. He did not wish for me to be hurt in any way. He stepped back and gave me ample space, careful to not influence my decision. He even attempted to walk away on a few occasions. He was willing to sacrifice love so that I could continue unfettered on the monastic journey.

In truth, the monastic vows we take are profound; they imprint an immutable awareness upon the soul, heart, and mind. For example, our initiation is made complete with our symbolic cremation performed by traditional priests. Familial name and title, birth status, inheritance and all other familial markings are ceremonially erased. With spiritual elders in tow, my initiation was performed on the banks of the holy River Ganges where I disrobed and offered my civilian apparel to the Mother River. Today, I stand unrobed again: This time, in the river of life as I relearn the cadence of an open world. My greatest strength to carry me through is love: I am both armed with and disarmed by love. The Seraph unrobed my heart. And now and forever I will be fortified by our eternal love.

FORGIVENESS & BLESSINGS

In early October, three months following the onset of my communication with the Seraph, I was well enough to set out on my difficult mission to India to see His Holiness, my Guru. How does one explain to their beloved teacher after thirty-six years of investment on the spiritual path—a path that whittles the psyche, mind, and soul into perfection with the knowledge of the Universe, God, and the Self—that one is no longer able to fasten oneself to that path? I was sad to face my teacher with this monumental decision. But I knew I had no choice. I knew that the sanctity of Self is not in the robes, or in a vow, as sacred an initiation as it is. Our spirituality lies in the integrity of Self—one that is sanctioned by the divine law of safeguarding the most important inheritance of life—love!

I knew my teacher would be saddened by my shocking and momentous decision. He had patiently mentored and nurtured me into knowledge; he had been a great and generous spiritual father to me. I am his progressive, radical daughter, but one he loves, nonetheless. I stumbled over my words as I tried to explain that the impossible had happened. My guru tried his best to persuade me to not renounce my vows. Although he was saddened by my decision, I held firm to my heart's condition. My heart was fully awakened and obviously my journey with my soul mate had not yet been completed. Karmas of the heart remained to be fulfilled. In renouncing my vow on the monastic path, I gained the chance to reclaim the freedom necessary to continue my journey into wholeness. I feel relieved to have executed the tenet by which I regained my spiritual freedom, while remaining open to spirit as I continue my journey of becoming Love.

Before leaving India to return home, I had one more special mission to perform. Following my meeting with His Holiness, I embarked on a most cherished trip from Coimbatore to Tiruvannamalai, a pilgrimage to this holy city in Tamil Nadu. It had been raining for days. The landscape was vibrant with life, birds joyfully tweeting ragas and ghazals. I love steam trains. I grew up with them and can still feel the deep serenity I felt as a child while traveling in the trains from New Amsterdam to Georgetown: The "*clack-a-lak-a-lak*" of the carriages brushing against the sweeping leaves of the banana groves as the train glides along the rails toward heaven. India's trains are magnificent and carefully managed; they recall that sense of nostalgia that goes beyond the coil of life. I loved being ensconced in the cozy carriages with the smell of fresh coffee, chai, and other vegetarian treats from vendors passing by with the titillating intonations of Tamil "mantras" as they announce their repast with repetitive rapidity. For instance, try repeating these words as fast as you can while intoning a lilting high-pitched inflection: "*chai, chai, chai, chai, chaaii*!" "*kapi, kapi, kapi, kapii*!" or "*vadaa, vadaa, vadaaaa*!"

As we pulled out of the bustling train station, I couldn't help but feel the fullness of heart with a renewed surge of freedom that harkened a new life and new beginnings. Heading to this major event to pay obeisance to the magnificent Lord Arunachala Shiva and the Goddess Mother Parvati would prove to be a seven-hour long journey to Light. My single-minded purpose on this pilgrimage was twofold in nature: to receive the blessings of Arunachala Shiva for me and my Seraph, and to seek permission of the Goddess Parvati for our renewed and auspicious life together, if this were to be the Divine Will. I also needed to perform spiritual austerities necessary for receiving the forgiveness of the God and Goddess for breaking my sacred vow as a Synnassin. For these reasons, I journeyed to the *Kartigai Dipam* (Hindu festival of light and love) that had just begun.

Kartigai Dipam is the oldest festival in South India. This observance falls in the Tamil month of *Kartigai* when the star *Kritigai* is on the ascendant, and usually occurs on a full moon day. The month of Kartigai is of special importance to Tamil people and derives its name from the star Kritigai (Scorpio). The sacred hamlet of Tiruvannamalai also happens to be the birthplace of the revered saint, Ramana Maharishi. Here I intended to reclaim a long forgotten treasure of the heart.

The way the chronicle of Arunachala Shiva is told by the Tamil scholars is as follows: Lord Shiva gave half his body to His Beloved Consort, Goddess Parvati, thereby uniting the Shiva and Shakti energies as One (Shiva-Shakti). As the legend goes, Goddess Parvati had taken refuge in these hills to perform certain extreme austerities to gain the love of Lord Shiva. The Saint, Gautama Muni, found Parvati while performing her *tapasya* and reported his sightings to Lord Shiva. Pleased with her sacrifice, Shiva came to Arunachala, recognized the Goddess as his Beloved Consort, and bequeathed half of his body to her.

Tiruvannamalai, the hill location of this story, also reveals the significance of Shiva's immense light. Lord Shiva asks Lord Brahma and Lord Vishnu to find out the exact location of his head and his feet. Since Lord Shiva's form is infinite, they were unable to find this locust. Lord Shiva revealed his cosmic powers by taking the form of a humongous beam of Light, *Jyoti*, on this hill. Here, in commemoration of this magnificent feat of light, a massive torch fueled by 3,500 kilos of ghee is lit on the zenith of the hill. It is said that Lord Shiva's infinite light is visible to devotees on this day. Millions of pilgrims from all over the world descend in this little hamlet to gain the blessings of Lord Shiva and the Goddess Parvati and to pay reverence to the Light of Love! The timing for my being at this momentous occasion was indeed fortuitous.

The sacred event generally lasts for nine days. I arrived on the third day of the festival after the crowds of a million or more had lessened to merely a few thousand local people. As soon as I arrived, I was told by my local friends, Vina and Sudhir (who were to be my guides on this pilgrimage), that I had brought the sunshine with me. Apparently, it had been raining since the onset of the festival and the humongous Dipam was hidden from view due to the fog and rain. That very afternoon, we started on our pilgrimage. We set out to walk the full perimeter of the mountain, some fourteen kilometers. The seasoned local pilgrims would walk this distance barefooted. Soaked in mud from the recent rains, the roadside was piled high with refuse left by the recent pilgrims. As we crossed the wet grassy patches and muddied earthen path, we climbed onto the official roadway that circumambulated the sacred hill. Because of the clear skies, we would be able to see the Dipam from every vantage point of the track when it became lit for the evening. The afternoon sun fell quickly in the Western sky and its huge golden-orange beams of light were penetrating a thin veil of fog hanging in the air. I could feel the residual energy of millions of pilgrims' prayers and intentions that had recently been uttered.

As I slipped into mantra mode, I noticed that even in my state of vulnerability (from having completed another round of invasive therapies), I felt my lungs filling with golden light and effulgent prana. At the halfway mark of the journey, I felt my feet barely touching ground as I floated forward with great momentum.

We took brief detours along the pilgrimage path to pay homage to deities of the eight cosmic directions. In tireless momentum, we maintained our stride while offering prayers and receiving blessings from each deity. Each shrine is presided by its own Shakti, or deity—the primordial force of each direction that is continually at work. The eight shrines are positioned at astronomically strategic locations along the path, each facing its intended cosmic direction. As a whole, these Shaktis represent the Cosmic Being, or *Vastu Purusha*. The deity for each direction offers specific boons.

PRIMORDIAL SPACE OF LOVE ~ EIGHT SHAKTIS

In Vedic knowledge of cosmic architecture, we cognize eight regents (*Astha Linga* or Eight Shaktis) that safeguard and sustain the collective space of love, nurturance, and life in our universe: My journey on this pilgrimage permitted me to enter this intricate vista of space where love is held in its immutable and pristine state. Although I am informed in the knowledge of the Vastu Purusha I was yet to glean a precise understanding of exactly how this operation impacts our human heart and sentiency.

As I made my way into the shrines, it was remarkable to witness my lungs becoming revived with each blessing. I felt my mind awaken with greater insights. Installed in the precise cosmic flow of the Creation, each shrine is situated along its particular energetic direction of the *Vastu Mandala*. Positioned in the very center of the energetic axis of the Vastu Mandala is the deity Brahma. This deity is responsible for issuing Primordial Desire, which creates manifestation and fuels love, just love! What is notable here is that, unlike the other Eight Shaktis, Brahma is not represented by a shrine. The plausible reason for this physical absence is that the central force of love is invisible, infinite, and immutable. It is this power which is forever divinizing the surrounding cosmic forces, or Shaktis, into the universal state of love. In turn, this state of love maintains the space of love within our hearts. This space of love is the center of our homes, center of our lives, and the center of our physical, emotional, and psychic bodies wherein the heart chakra lies. Love is dynamically positioned in the epicenter of our being. It is this love that is the absolute source of everything. It is the central wellspring of cosmic memory that sustains life. It is the maternal core of universal energy from which all other energies are sourced. As such, it protects, nourishes, and keeps alive the foundational intelligence responsible for manifestation and consciousness.

Here are the Eight Shaktis (the cosmic memory and foundational energies of the universe), which safeguard the physical world as well as our individual awareness, and which are held together by Love.

Indra—Eastward Direction—Lord of the Firmament—responsible for overseeing the affairs of the world and their successful outcome.

Agni—Southeast Direction—Lord of Fire— responsible for generating energy and bestowal of health and wellness.

Yama—South Direction—Lord of Death—responsible for recycling rebirths and balancing individual karmas and debts.

Nirtti—Southwest Direction—Keeper of Ancestral History—responsible for the resolve of negative emotions and actions.

Varuna—West Direction—Lord of Water—responsible for sustenance and social development.

Vayu—Northwest Direction—Lord of the Winds—responsible for movement and disseminating information.

Kubera—North Direction—Lord of Wealth—responsible for economic and financial wellness.

Ishana—Northeast Direction—Lord of All Quarters of the Universe—responsible for safeguarding the meditative mind and individual awareness.

MOTHER'S SHAKTI ~ SHIVA'S LOVE

Just a ways beyond the halfway mark of my pilgrimage route, dusk descended. The stupendous Dipam at the center of the hilltop was lit for the evening. Its brilliant glow illumined the sky as my companions and I stopped to pay reverence to the glow of Shiva's Light atop the hill. We sat for a brief while as Vina explained that it had been the first time since the festival began that the Dipam was visible from all corners of the path. I could see the light clearly. To me, this was a powerful indication that I was forgiven by Shiva's Light for breaking my vows, and that the new path ahead of me would be clearly lit and free from obstacles. As we continued onward, I decided to disband my shoes. At first it was painful walking barefooted on the pebbled road, but after a while I felt nothing, only the pleasant coolness of the muddied path under my feet.

Suddenly, I became aware that there was a procession ahead of us. It had stopped on the pilgrim's route amid the imperceptible hush of excitement and exuberance from a smattering of pilgrims. As we neared the stopped procession, Sudhir exclaimed in awe, "It's the motorcade of the Goddess Mother!" She is called Annamalai on this occasion, another name for Goddess Parvati. Dressed up in splendid regalia and mounted on a throne, she is carried on a stupendous golden chariot built for the purpose of perambulating the fourteen kilometers of sacred ground. With priests and tenders in tow and puja lamps, incense, and oil torches ablaze, it was indeed a spectacular sight to behold. We were stunned to see such a small number of pilgrims and villagers lining the path to receive the Goddess's potent blessings as she passed their way. A climactic event of the festival, the Goddess's procession would normally be flanked by hundreds of thousands of pilgrims striving to get near enough to catch a glimpse of her!

Apparently, the procession had left early that morning from Arunachaleshwara Temple where it had originated. This temple is the central locust of operation for this festival. The Goddess's motorcade was to have completed its perambulation by noon that day, hours before we had embarked onto the track. But as fate would have it, the procession was delayed on its outbound journey and, for no apparent reason, had been stopped halfway around the pilgrim's path. And there we were within a few feet of the Goddess Mother. I came to a stop within a foot's proximity of the Goddess and stood there facing her in silent prayer. I prayed for guidance and for the welfare of my Beloved Seraph. I asked to be shown a sign: Was it in the Divine Plan for me to walk this life's journey with my Seraph? And will we achieve happiness and harmony on our life path together? Suddenly, I heard a car stopping on the roadside by the chariot. As I opened my eyes, someone reached out to receive the priest's blessings. (That was strange since no vehicles were allowed onto this juncture of the path.) The priest then turned to me and beckoned me forward to receive blessings. He poured blessed water over my head, circled the *dhupam* in my face, and gave me the blessings of *kum kum* in my hand. As other pilgrims reached out for blessings, he did not move, nor did he beckon to anyone else. Suspended in the Mother's light and holding back the tears, I bowed in humble obeisance to her. It was a significant sign that my new movement forward is the rightful path for me, and that my Seraph and I will always be held in the Mother Goddess's profound blessings.

Having secured her Darshana, the next scheduled stop was Arunachaleswara Temple where I hoped to gain the blessings of Lord Shiva. To avoid the crowds, Vina and I started out early the next morning to this magnificent temple. This sanctum holds the great heart of Shiva—it being the historic locust where he and Goddess Parvati became enjoined. This union issued forth the Primordial Oneness we have come to know as Shiva-Shakti. Shiva represents the absolute immutable energy behind the creation, while Shakti is the apparent dynamic energy that is imperative for manifestation, preservation, and dissolution of the universe. Here I sought the forgiveness of Arunachala Shiva. I needed to re-secure Shiva's blessings and ask him to sanction the love I bear for my Seraph.

As Vina and I arrived at the temple, there were already thousands of devotees in line waiting to purchase tickets to gain entry. I felt dismayed and began to wonder whether accessibility to Shiva might prove difficult. Suddenly, I looked up and saw a flock of white geese circling the open skies above the temple courtyard. For me, it was a sign that we would be allowed entry. No sooner had I given birth to this thought when I noticed a guard sitting behind a window in a closed ticket booth on the other side of the long cue. I asked Vina to go up to him and let him know that we had traveled from afar and wished to gain a faster track into the temple. Vina was not very hopeful, but went up to the window nonetheless. The moment we approached the guard, he immediately sought another guard to whisk us directly into the temple's sanctum! Although one may gain access into the temple, very few are permitted to enter the actual sanctum. Ushered through circuitous hidden passageways, we were led directly into Shiva's sanctum.

In this ancient sanctum sat the most beautiful idol of Lord Shiva, dressed in full regalia while being supplicated in ceremonial abundance by four awesome Tamil priests. As we entered, a few devotees were being blessed inside the sanctum. Much to my glee, the main priest beckoned me forward to sit in the cleared center space. There I prostrated and fell into a timeless spell at the feet of Shiva. The priest requested my *gotra* (family lineage) and *nakshatra* (lunar mansion) and immediately proceeded to perform a special puja for me. During this time, I felt my mind crystallize; I saw the colors of the aurora borealis and I kept my intention for receiving Shiva's blessing for me and my Seraph in pure focus. His sublime blessing resounded in the powerful vibration of Tamil priests' voices as they chanted in silvery tones attuned to the resonance of the puja bells. The brilliance of massive ghee lamps splayed my vision as the opulent fragrance of Indian jasmine, myrrh, sandalwood, and rose permeated the sanctum. I heard the inner voice gleefully recalling a line I had written for me and my Seraph, "Let the gentle whisper of our soulful reunion be heard by all the worlds!" As the priest echoed "Om Tat Sat!" (So it shall be!), he handed me abundant *prasadam* (holy sacraments) from the puja. With my mind in a trance, and knees wobbly, I understood that Shiva's Blessing would be with us for eternity.

Before leaving Tiruvannamalai by train that evening, I paid a brief visit to the tranquil ashram abode of the saint Ramana Maharishi. There I was privileged to visit the Goushala (abode of the cows) and met with a most enchanting sight. Two calves were birthed that morning; one was fawn colored and the other was onyx black with a white spot on its forehead in the shape of a perfect heart. As I stood in the doorway of the Goushala, the black calf wobbled over to me; I bent and stroke its beautiful head. The response was a very wet kiss on my face.

My Seraph is never far away. I use the sacred act of divination to commune with him. Every tree, wind, winged creature, every movement and every raindrop, each speck of light tells me what I need to know—his welfare, challenges, happiness, grief, or joy. The forest that bears the fruit of love which swells inside of him; the wind that rides upon my heart and travels to him;

the river that flows and whets my thoughts of him; the sky that spans the eternity of love I bear for him; the cosmic breath that tunes the thousand strings my heart plays for him; the mind of radiant light streaming with the oneness of love, I carry him. O, these are the timeless ways by which we shall forever touch upon that luminous soul.

With Divine Grace at work, I am happy to flow in grace and allow spirit to reveal itself. I trust the universe to do what is meant to be done. The Seraph and I are one soul indivisible, mirroring each other. Whatever he sees in me, I see in him. It is this connection that continually rescues us with an outpouring of love from an awakened heart.

Love! Just Love

Love is sanctioned by the heavens
as the blissful law of earth.

The infinite equation of love:
one plus one equals One.

Love's beautiful memory is
gentle and fragile,
exuding barely a whisper like the
glistening wings of white butterflies or
the imperceptible light of dawn gliding
seamlessly across an invisible sky.

The fundamental qualities of
spiritual life are to love, nourish,
nurture, and heal.

Love's infinite trust is made secure by prayer ~
a faith that is rooted in the Divine and
not in the promise of this world.

When the journey is love and the
destination is love, where else can we go?

Love flourishes in serenity ~
a condition cultivated by trust and faith.

Love, trust, and heal thyself ~ the music of
heaven is heard everywhere love exists.

Let us not mourn our tears.
They flow from the heart of love to
water the arid soil of the soul.

The journey to the heart is the
shortest distance of all journeys, yet it
takes us the longest time to reach.

Love is our true nature.
All else is what we impose upon it.

Prayer is love! It realizes the greatest
good by nourishing desires
of the heart and healing the troubled mind.
It unfolds the present and
future with kindness.

Conscience is the heart's refraction
of light upon the mind.
May your thoughts flow in harmony
with your actions.

I exist in love for you whom I exist.

The Sanskrit word for "heart" is Hrdaya.
Hri means "to give," Da, "to receive,"
and Ya, "to move in harmony."
Keeping a balance of these three actions
is what love's about.

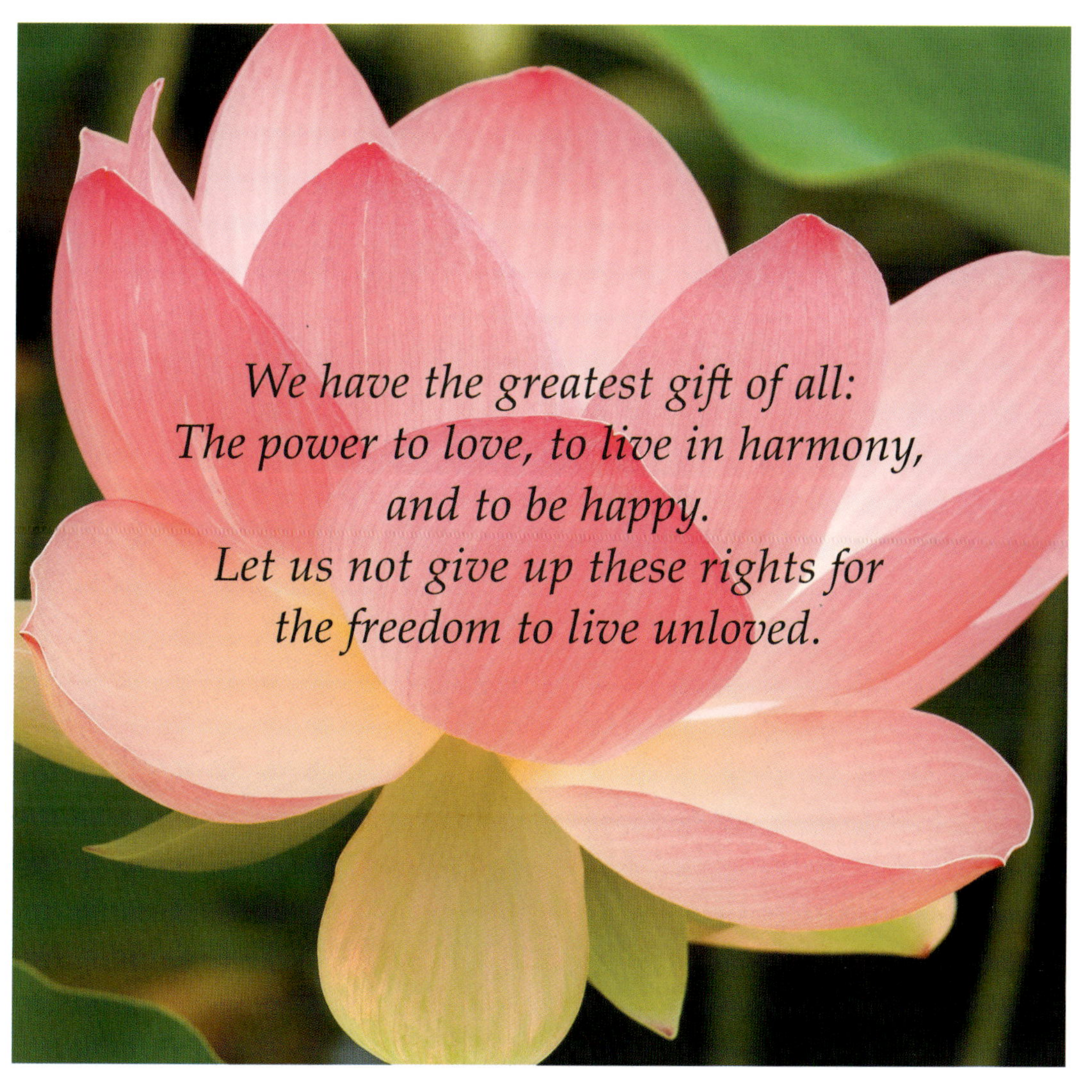
We have the greatest gift of all:
The power to love, to live in harmony,
and to be happy.
Let us not give up these rights for
the freedom to live unloved.

May your inner light grow brightly to
awaken the mind of awareness, the heart
of love, and the soul of compassion.

If I could give you only one gift,
it would be to take a chance with love.
You'll never lose!

Withdraw, heal, and focus your love
in moving smoothly through the here and now.
Know the future will take care of itself.

Love opens every door, attracts everything we need, and endows immeasurable happiness.

Let each and every breath restore a trail of harmony, happiness, and love.

Each moment, I send you light.
Every minute, a prayer.
Every second, my infinite love.

Neither distance nor time can erase
love when it is rooted in Divine faith.

Be still like the lotus and the deer,
the sky and the grasses.
Allow faith to grow and secure love.

Enter the realm of love where flaws
become faultless, where there is
room only for love and light.

The lotus retreats into her womb of night
to replenish the soul of light. Be like the lotus.

Love transforms darkness.
It is the light that heals all. Heal.

The heart knows
its content of love
and leaps in
exaltation with
love's fulfillment.

Take courage and surrender to love
by removing safety nets and escape hatches.

The sun is the everlasting reminder that each and every moment we gain renewed power to transcend our old selves.

Create harmony around you by investing in the sacred energy of kindness and you will find love surrounding you.

Here and now, initiate a commitment to
inner harmony, and you will intuitively
move away from anything that creates conflict
and disturbs your peace.

Freedom of spirit comes from the depth of happiness we rescue from the mire of life.

Inner freedom is secured once we achieve
the full measure of happiness in life.

*Love is never fulfilled by expectations
we project onto it. Love is fed and nurtured
only by endless acts of sacrifice and grace.*

Let silence illumine the spaces within
so its light can travel to those cells
that are challenged by disease or despair.

Let your commitment to inner harmony
be the filter through which
you respond to all things.

Let your inner light blaze and all
else will reflect harmony.

Love's intimacy melts away the physical world.
Be at one with love.

I cannot bear to be estranged from the
reservoir of love ~ not for a single moment.

Live your Ahimsa!
Focus your day on becoming the
instrument that dissolves disharmony
and despair into harmony and hope.

My healing and your healing is a
pervasive energy that instantly touches
the immutable soul of the entire family,
community, humanity, and world.

Take pause; allow your thoughts to settle;
refill love from within.

The practice of peace is the most positive act
you can invoke in your life right now.

Love's brilliant luminosity ensues when you fast
the mind of negative thoughts and emotions.

When love starts to wane, take pause!
Sit in yourself and allow silence to replenish spirit.

If circumstance should cast doubt
on the authenticity of love,
keep prayer alive. The Divine Light
illuminates our way to truth.

When in doubt with love, pursue its logic:
Listen to your heart.

Prayer for revelation and resolve is
a potent balm for the spirit.

Nothing is more present than the
radiant harmony of the rising sun
on the stillness of mind.
Awaken. Breathe. Be Aware.

Each one of us possesses the unassailable
power to whittle away our karmic imprints
and make luminous the wondrous spirit.

The heart mourns when we allow its radiant love
to shrivel away with longings and obsession.

When we feel we've lost everything, or
suffer from any "loss," we are only reminded
that what was lost was never ours
to lose in the first place.

Specks of light,
two thousand stars,
spatter the pathway.
Have a peaceful day.

Intimacy with the Divine arises
from the small acts
of kindness we express each day.

*Humor is the balm of wisdom
for healing old wounds.*

It is from the heart of faith
that serenity begins.

Laughter is a gift to and from the Divinity.

*Mellow is the memory of distant time,
like fine rays of the departing sun filtering
through the feathery destiny of clouds and
fluttering on the memory strings of the heart.*

Serene is the heart that is filled with joy;
a faith that knows pain yet can still endure.

The path of healing
is a great place to
ignite our sense of humor.

The heart is not a cremation ground to
burn the toxic waste of the past.
It is the initiator of eternal light,
the never-ending Divinity.

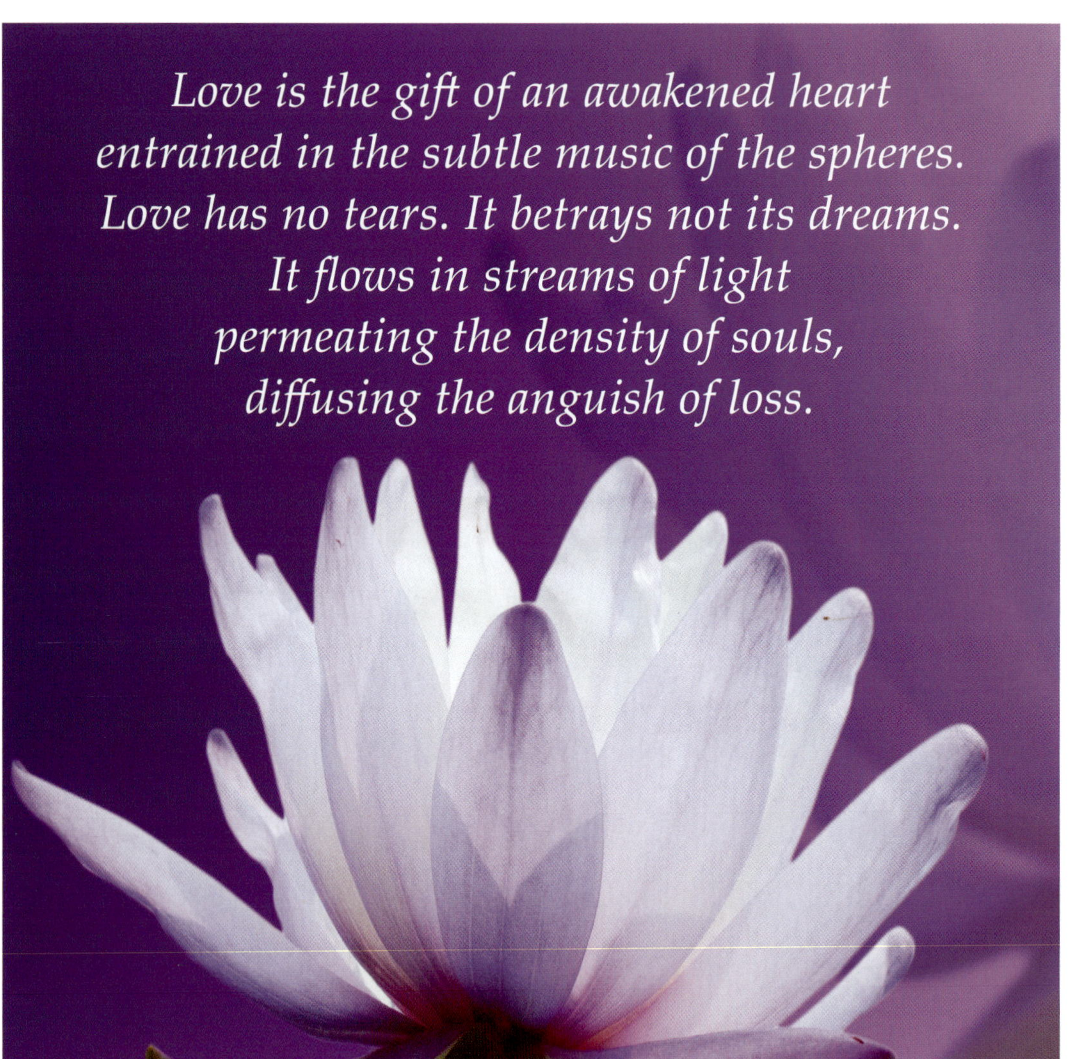
Love is the gift of an awakened heart
entrained in the subtle music of the spheres.
Love has no tears. It betrays not its dreams.
It flows in streams of light
permeating the density of souls,
diffusing the anguish of loss.

A river of tears is generously gifted
to cleanse and nourish the heart.

O Sun, your vibration retunes the refrain
of the heart, each ray transporting
a splendid melody ~ loving without end.

Trust Love. Let your presence be
where your heart is.

Peace ~ Love ~ Light. It is that simple.

To find your soul mate, call upon your
greater self and say, "Come and share
the Divine Grace with me, my love!"

I will my love to Thy Will.

Throughout your day remember this:
I love you because I am love.

Love never turns cold.
It exudes warmth through the memory
of having loved.

Love is unbreakable.
It does not shatter because relationships fall apart.

We shall not die for love.
It is not within human design
to choose life or death.
We shall not cry for love.
It is not a cremation ground to be mourned.
We shall not fight for love.
It is not a battlefield to sacrifice the heart.
We shall celebrate love
and its eternal power to foist sweetness
onto the parched earth of the heart
and the dust of the mind.

*Love is a spiritual reality.
Happiness is a spiritual experience.*

Nature is spiritual.
Life is spiritual.
Love is spiritual.

*Spirituality is about feasting our
spirit with love and kindness.*

When you heal, the family heals.
When the family heals, the community heals.
When the community is healed and happy,
the earth celebrates.
Commit yourself to healing.

Climb to the mountaintop,
soar with winged creatures,
watch the broken heart
of the sky peeping through
its stars, and heal.

Love flourishes when we
hone our ability to see deeply
into the nature of things.

"Spiritual" is what "sacred"
becomes once it is transformed
through the power
of our awareness.

Love and happiness are the
natural results of awakening
to our spirituality.

The eyes of love give vision to the soul and words to the heart.

Practice the act of abundant gratitude
for the plants, animals, trees, rivers, sky, and
earth, and the Divine mystery that is
Love will be revealed.

Express love in your thoughts, speech,
and action, and you will become Love.

I can exist without my religion,
my peers, and my followers,
but I cannot survive without love.

The greatest temple in all the world lies
within the Self. It is called Love.

The special heart I bear for you is greater
than the wealth of the whole universe.

Love is the soul, the core energy of spirit.

Invest in faith and the religion of love will follow.

Life sketches itself into memory and character. The deeper the etchings, the more spiritual we become.

My human experience is tantamount
to the love I bear for thee.

*We are spiritual beings living
a human experience.*

It is awakening to our profound nature
of love that makes us spiritual.

Spirituality is rarely what we
think it is. It is about the awareness
to see clearly, live peacefully, and
to grow our wealth of love.

Let us recapture our sense of vigor, vitality, and wholeness by occasionally fasting from food, noise, worries, and people.

Be in the motion of love in and
through everything you do.

Because we are composed of love,
we have the infinite power to create
and recreate love through each and
every breath and movement.

Love expresses itself in subtle ways ~
like the calmness of winter's moon and
vibrancy of summer's dawn.

*Healing is the ongoing ebb
and flow of life ~
you are healing at all times.*

The boon of love is to experience love.
The bane of love is to expect love.

Bask in the sunlight. Let it be where it is.
See the deer in the forest.
Let them be where they are.
Sit in yourself and simply be.

Love, when brimming with fullness,
is your greatest medicine.

Let my love be the safe haven
for you while everything else
evolves and resolves in its own time.

Laughter, when you
have no reason to laugh,
is in fact, a good
reason to laugh.

Laugh when you are sad.
Laugh when you are happy.
Laugh because you feel unloved.
Laugh because you are loved.

Gleefully shout out your laughter.
It is potent Inner Medicine.

What we love becomes
a vital part of our life force,
immunity, soul, and destiny.

Hope is the elixir of life.
Hope means love is alive!

We don't experience the fullness of love
when we impose strictures upon it.

Love is immortal. Love heals.
Love nourishes.

I am sacred. You are sacred.
The "sacred" simply is.

*At vulnerable times seek out
a private space within; be sparse.
Let love and light in.*

Love is the authentic expression of our soul.
Be in integrity with love.

The object of love is the subject of love.

Love shared is wealth invested.

Love, like happiness,
is a spiritual journey
that requires
your courage.

Love perishes from blind actions and betrayals.

Love flourishes with
thoughtfulness and kindness.

To preserve love we must resolve
disharmony into a state of joy.

There can be no harmony within
or peace in the world until
we cultivate the mentality of love.
For this we must stop the hurting.

Strive to safeguard inner harmony.
It is your most precious wealth.

When you live to honor love, every tissue,
cell, and memory of your heart becomes
divinized with prayer.

Love, having filled the heart, spills forth
wit and wisdom, laughter and exuberance.

Science has yet to
discover that each
cell within your
heart contains the
universe's memory
of love. Let your
eternal memory of
love guide you.

Love filters through the heart like the constant sun illuminates the earth.

*Let love permeate your heart
and keep you whole.*

The Mother is the cosmic law on earth.
She is the infinite force of maternal love.

Love given is mirrored a
thousand-fold within and around you.

Love is not for, with, or about another person.
It is the content of consciousness
within your heart. When awakened it
brightens up the whole world.

Love cannot be expressed by emotions or words.
It comes alive through our actions.

Healing is a reality that is happening in every moment of our lives if we are aware of it.

A mind poised in awareness recognizes
the Self and Nature to be One Love.

The greatest wisdom is held in love,
the greatest love is found in compassion.

The Mother's infinite reservoir of love
is the safe space where you can resolve
worries, concerns, hurt, and angst.

All of Nature is created and sustained
by the cosmic principle of Love.

Once you become lit from within,
you attract more love and happiness to you.

Pursue light
and you will
find love!

Love rescues and nourishes
the sacredness of heart.

Live in a house full of light.
The best room in the house is the
heart filled with love.

What is love, but light you
cultivate to illumine a peaceful heart!

It's a glorious day!
Breathe in joy,
breathe out worries.
Live your love.

Our human organism is cosmically
programmed to continually rekindle light.

Pure love travels faster than the speed of light.
Broadcast love to your past,
present, and future.

Purity of heart inspires love and fosters wisdom.

Your heart is pure.
It has the power to transmit light into
the pristine waters of your soul.

A life force affirmation for the day:
I seek to preserve the prana of life that is love.

Love lifts me up to greater heights
to touch the stars in heaven.

If by chance we do not manifest
our soul mate in this lifetime,
we're already fulfilled by knowing love.

Today, I offer my gratitude to the Divine
for the boundless energy of love
sent me to heal and be whole again.

You are the immutable spirit,
imbued with the awesome
power to create love.

Let your heart be like
a lotus that blooms with
every kindness.

*Beauty is fed, nurtured, and
nourished only by love.*

To replenish the dream,take a journey into
the cosseted womb of night. Take rest!

I am Love. You are Love.
We are One Love.

Even the finest ray of light can
produce unbounded hope,
which rapidly converts into more light.

Hope must never perish.
It ripples through spirit
like sunlight on water
making fresh the mind and
luminous the heart.

Our human organism is cosmically
programmed to continually rekindle light.

*Love is a perennial education,
a progressive awareness of who we are
and how we respond to life.*

*There are times when the heart
and mind become lonely.
Eat lightly, take brisk walks, soak your feet
in the cool springs, and breathe.*

We are Innocence, because
our core nature is that of love.

Awaken your heart and
you will need no other light.

Open your heart to light
and all shadows fall behind you.

Love grows and evolves on a mountain
of memories, past and present.
It builds a bridge that crosses the
pathway into the heavens.

Desires and expectations can break
the heart, but love mends it.

It is only through facing our imperfections
that we can reorder and strengthen love.

What good are fame, wealth, and power
if they stand in the way of our freedom
to love and live happily?

Love is a timeless journey.
It has no goodbyes, farewells, or hellos.

My unconditional love for you
has but one condition: your happiness.

*Let's not confuse "love" with "desire"
~ one is eternal, the other ephemeral.*

In true love desires and needs
are invariably mutual.

If you find that a dream has ended, then the awakening of the heart has begun for the real dream to take form.

It is infinitely fulfilling to behold that which exudes beauty, gentleness, and nurturance.

We must never flinch from the anchor of hope.

Love is the dominant cosmic force of Nature
that is energy, the Shakti that generates life.

Each and every moment,
love creates an opportunity for us to
be mended into wholeness.

Like a tender vine bearing the full weight
of its fruits, let your hearts be entwined
as One to nourish everlasting love.

Wisdom transforms a challenge into a teaching ~
it teaches the heart to learn and trust through love.

Life has destined for us one true path ~
to live in harmony and integrity with all things.

Harmony is the foundation
on which love grows.
Disharmony erodes love.

Silence is the reservoir of our wellness,
the reflection of a contented heart.
Have you practiced silence lately?

What is eternal love but the light of awareness
that illumines the heart to awaken?

Love becomes deeper, more profound,
as your power of awareness grows.

*Love is subtle. It is an invisible energy
that pervades each and every breath,
thought, and movement.*

Love nourishes one billion times greater than any other means of sustenance on earth.

Love is the natural order
of the universe.

Be swelled my love, by love.

Open your heart to compassion
and there you will find love!

Love! First, last, and always.

My Seraph unrobed my heart.
And I stand naked in the cosmos of eternal love.